Quiz No 212998
Moonfleet

Warburton, Nick
B.L.: 3.7
Points: 1.0   MY

Moo

J. Meade Falkner

Adapted by Nick Warburton

Illustrated by Mark Oldroyd

OXFORD
UNIVERSITY PRESS

Contents

Chapter 1: Blackbeard's ghost   5

Chapter 2: A warning   16

Chapter 3: Underground   22

Chapter 4: Homeless   30

Chapter 5: A puzzle solved   46

Chapter 6: Deep in the castle   52

Chapter 7: Stolen!   63

Chapter 8: Paying the price   70

CHAPTER I

---◆---

Blackbeard's ghost

My name is John Trenchard, and this is the
story of my journey across the sea and through
many dangers. It started when I was a boy in the
village of Moonfleet in the County of Dorset.

When I look back now I can see myself,
wide-awake in my aunt's cottage, listening to
the roar of the sea. The waves are pounding the
beach down on the shore. I am safe in bed, but I
know some poor ship is out in Moonfleet bay.

I close my eyes and imagine that ship. The
storm is tossing it about like a toy. It is driving it
aground.* Then I hear other sounds. There are
voices, shouting in the wind. The men of the
village are running down to the beach, ready

to risk their lives for the poor souls on that wrecked ship.

Of course, it wasn't always stormy in Moonfleet. On some nights, the sea was calm and there was no moon. That's when the smugglers* went to work. I used to lie in my bed and imagine the smugglers too.

I used to imagine a smugglers' ship out in the bay. It sails in silently and drops anchor. Barrels are unloaded, and there are men and horses waiting on the beach to carry them off into the dark.

Smuggling was secret work and I wasn't supposed to know about it. Folk were poor in Moonfleet. Sometimes they broke the law so they could afford to eat. But they weren't bad. They were the same men who risked their lives for shipwrecked sailors.

If ever the magistrate* heard what the smugglers were up to, he sent men from the Revenue* out to stop them. Then there would be soldiers running along the cliff tops, or putting out in a boat to chase them. You might hear a cry ring out over the bay: 'Smugglers! In the name of the king, give yourselves up!'

In those days, when I was a boy, the magistrate was a bitter, cruel man named Maskew. He didn't know it, but Maskew was the reason I had to leave my home in Moonfleet and start on my journey.

My story starts late one evening, in the October of 1757, when I was walking through Moonfleet churchyard. I came across Master Ratsey carving letters on a tombstone.

'Come over here, John,' he called to me. 'Hold up the lantern so I can see to get this finished.'

I did as he asked and held the lantern for him. I saw what he was carving. It was a poem for a boy from the village, David Block. David was a boy about my age. He had been out on a boat with the smugglers one night when the Revenue men turned up. They gave chase and the boy was shot and killed.

'It was a cruel thing to fire on so young a lad,' said Ratsey, as he worked at the stone.

'Who fired the gun?' I asked.

Ratsey lowered his voice. 'They say it was Magistrate Maskew.'

'And who wrote the poem?'

'Parson* Glennie.'

The poem was a bold one. It said the man who killed young David was heartless and one day he would answer for his actions.

'Then Mr Glennie's a brave man,' I said. 'Maskew won't like these words.'

'He won't,' said Ratsey, 'and he's not meant to.'

When the tombstone was finished, Ratsey took me to the inn. Everyone in Moonfleet called this inn the *Why Not?*, but its real name was the *Mohune Arms*. The Mohunes were once a powerful Dorset family. They had owned the inn and all of Moonfleet. That's where the name comes from. You could still see their coat of arms* over the fireplace – a carved shield with a black 'Y' on it.

You couldn't find Mohunes in the village any

more. They lost all their money, and all that was left of them then was the name – Moonfleet – and that letter 'Y' in the shield. So folk in the village called the inn the *Why Not?* as a joke, and the name stuck.

I was nervous about going inside so I hesitated at the door. My aunt did not like the place. She said only wicked people ever went there. She was a sharp woman and she didn't care much for me. Sometimes I thought she was just waiting for an excuse to send me away.

'Don't worry, John,' said Ratsey. 'I shan't tell her.'

But still I hesitated.

'What now?'

'The innkeeper,' I said. 'He…he always looks so grim.'

I often saw him in the village, and I thought he didn't like me. His name was Elzevir Block. It was his son, David, who'd been killed by the Revenue.

'Elzevir is sad,' said Ratsey. 'So he needs friends to cheer him up, doesn't he? Don't worry about Elzevir Block, boy. There never was a better man in Moonfleet.'

So I took Ratsey at his word and we went into the *Why Not?* together.

Elzevir Block was sitting in a chair, looking into the fire. He had a shock of grey hair, and he was thickset and very strong. He looked up at us. 'What does this boy want?'

'The same as me, Elzevir. A warm drink to keep off the chill. He was hanging around the churchyard and he helped me finish David's tombstone. May the poor lad rest in peace.'

'Ay, he does rest in peace,' said the innkeeper. 'But those who killed him will never rest in peace when their time comes. And it may come sooner than they think.'

'You be careful what you say, Elzevir,' said Ratsey. 'These days it's not safe to speak your mind in Moonfleet.'

Then Ratsey got out the board and we played a game of backgammon* until it was late and he realised my aunt would be angry.

'Hurry, John,' he said. 'That aunt of yours is strict, remember.'

'Yes, you must hurry home,' said Elzevir. 'Men say that the ghost of Blackbeard walks on the first nights of winter.'

'That's right,' said Ratsey, almost whispering. 'Blackbeard. Some say they've met him face to face.'

I glanced at the window but it was dark outside.

'But that's only talk,' I said. 'Isn't it?'

'Talk, is it?' Elzevir said, leaning closer. 'Didn't you hear about Cracky Jones?'

I nodded. Yes, I had heard. Cracky Jones was a poor mad boy, found dead in the churchyard.

'They say he saw Blackbeard, and heard him calling,' said Ratsey.

I began to fear the short walk back to my aunt's cottage. I would have to go by the churchyard. And I knew as well as anyone that old Colonel Mohune, known as Blackbeard, was buried under the church a hundred years ago.

'Oh, he's still seen,' said Ratsey, his eyes shining. 'Men have seen him by the light of an old lantern. He has a full black beard and a coppery face. So they say.'

The story was that Blackbeard was searching
for his treasure in the churchyard. He was the
worst of all the Mohunes, was Blackbeard. He
fought in the Civil War between King Charles
and Cromwell, changing sides whenever
it suited him. When he was Governor of
Carisbrooke Castle, on the Isle of Wight, he had
to guard King Charles himself, and that was how

he came by his treasure.

'What was his treasure?' I asked.

'A great diamond,' Ratsey said. 'The King promised it to Blackbeard if he'd help him to escape from the castle.'

'And did he escape?'

'No. Blackbeard took the diamond and then warned the soldiers.'

'So he cheated?'

'He did. He kept the diamond and hid it somewhere. But he died soon afterwards. They say that the diamond has a curse on it. Anyway, it's never been seen since.'

Then Elzevir jumped up and said it was time to lock the doors. He told me to hurry home and to mind how I went as I passed the church.

I ran through the dark as fast as I could and I was out of breath when I got to my aunt's cottage.

I saw no sign of Blackbeard on the way, though. At least, I saw no sign of him on that night. I was going to meet the terrible Colonel Mohune, and soon enough, but I didn't know it then.

CHAPTER 2

A warning

A few nights later, the wind got up and we could tell that a storm was on its way. Thatch came flying from the roofs and the rain was so bad that the churchyard was flooded. The church itself was left like a steep little island. It was hard to get there for the Sunday service and when we did we found streamers of seaweed caught on the tombstones.

That morning, during the service, a strange thing happened. Just as Mr Glennie, the parson, stood up to speak, a deep booming sound echoed round the church.

'What was that?' I whispered to Ratsey.

He only shook his head and told me to listen

to Mr Glennie. But I heard the same sound again, and this time I was sure it came from somewhere underneath the church. I forgot about Mr Glennie and listened hard.

There it was again! A deep, slow knocking sound. And no one said a word about it.

I began to think I was imagining it until an old lady sitting at the back of the church jumped up and called out, 'Can't you hear it? It's the Mohunes rising from their graves!'

'Please, Mrs Tucker, sit down,' the parson said. 'There's nothing to be afraid of.'

But that unearthly* noise had frightened her. She would not sit down, and ran out of the church. That made me even more uneasy, and I began to imagine all sorts of things. There was a simple reason for it, though, and Mr Glennie gave it to me after the service.

He said that under the church was a vault, like a huge cave. The floods had filled the vault and set the coffins afloat. They were bumping into one another. That was all.

I felt relieved until I saw Ratsey shaking his head again.

'Oh no,' he said. 'That's more than coffins afloat – it's a warning.'

'A warning?' said Mr Glennie. 'No, Ratsey, that's silly talk.'

Ratsey said he knew it was a warning.

'What sort of warning?'

'To young lads,' he said. 'To keep away from what isn't their business.' And he stared at me.

It made me shiver to think of the Mohunes down there in the dark. And Blackbeard himself in the biggest coffin of all, crashing into the others.

But the sound we heard in church was hard, and made by solid, new wood. Not old coffins. So, if it wasn't coffins, what on earth was it?

The next day I went back to the church to see if I could still hear the noise. I was surprised to see Ratsey and Elzevir Block there ahead of me. Ratsey was lying on the ground with his ear to the wall. When he saw me he scrambled to his feet.

'I was looking at the wall,' he said awkwardly, 'to see if it needs any work after the floods. Will you run back to my workshop, John, and fetch my plasterer's hammer?'

I did as he asked, but when I came back, he looked embarrassed and said he didn't need the hammer after all. I glanced at Elzevir and saw his eyes twinkle under heavy brows.

They were hiding something from me, I was sure. It was something to do with the church and that strange sound. What was it?

Parson Glennie was also our schoolmaster. He was a kind-hearted man, and I enjoyed his lessons.

I also liked going to school to see Grace Maskew, the magistrate's daughter, with her thin face and tangle of light brown hair. She could run faster than most of the boys, and was very popular. I suppose I always admired Grace. I thought of her as a good friend, even though her father had killed David Block.

Maskew was a lawyer from Scotland. He was a rich man, and he and Grace lived in the Manor House. Her mother had died many years before.

All Moonfleet hated the magistrate but Grace we liked, and no one said a word against her father when she was near.

One day, while we were working in school, we heard the door open. We looked round and there stood Maskew. He looked angry. I could tell he'd been to the market because he carried a basket with a large fish in it.

We knew there was trouble in the air. Grace said nothing and looked down at her desk. Mr Glennie's face turned pale, but he smiled and wished Maskew a good day.

'I've seen it, Parson,' Maskew said, marching up to him. 'I've seen your words on that young rogue's tombstone.'

Mr Glennie started to mumble a reply but Maskew cut him off. 'Grace! Get your cape and come with me. I won't have you go to a school where the teacher calls me murderer.' He pointed a bony finger at Mr Glennie. 'Get rid of that stone, Parson, or I'll have it smashed to pieces.'

'Mr Maskew, you can't do that…'

'Don't you dare tell me what I can't do!'

Then Maskew snatched the fish from his basket and hit Mr Glennie in the face with it. It was a cowardly blow and, worse than that, it made us children laugh. I'm ashamed to say I laughed with them. Then I saw Mr Glennie's pale, hurt face and I was bitterly sorry.

Grace did not come to our little school after that. I never forgot her, though. And I know she thought of me. I know she did because, much later, it was Grace Maskew who helped to save my life.

CHAPTER 3

Underground

In time the floods dried up, but they left their
mark. In places the ground was cracked and
weakened. I was walking through the
churchyard one afternoon when I heard a
rumbling and a crumbling beneath my feet.
I looked down and saw a huge crack in the
path, near the base of a large tomb. It was
wide enough for a lad like me to slip inside. I
hesitated. But then I couldn't resist the chance to
find out what was down there. So I slithered in.

To my surprise, I found I was in a dark passage
right under the path. It sloped gently down
towards the church. The first thing I thought
of was the story of Blackbeard, hunting for his

diamond. Perhaps I'd found the passage that would lead me to it.

I made up my mind to return that same night, and bring a candle, so I could see what was hidden down that passage.

I went to bed that night and waited, wide-awake, for darkness to come. When I was sure my aunt was asleep, I took a candle and the tinderbox* and crept out of the house. It was deep into the night by then.

When I came to the dark shape of the church, my nerve failed me, just for a moment. In my mind I could see a tall figure, hairy and evil-looking, springing from the shadow of the church. It was almost enough to send me running home. But I thought of Blackbeard's diamond, and took a deep breath and on I went.

I found the crack in the earth and climbed into the passage underneath without any trouble. There I lit the candle and I could see an earthy tunnel ahead of me.

I began to walk along it, whistling to keep my courage up. After a while I came to a stone wall. I guessed it was the church wall. It was broken through to make a ragged doorway into a large room. I stepped through and looked around.

I was now right under the church. All around the sides of the room were stone shelves, and on the shelves stood coffins. Yes, this was the Mohune vault!

But coffins weren't the only things in the vault. In the middle of this room scores of barrels were stacked together. This must be where the smugglers kept their loot! So that was what caused the noise in church. It was barrels bumping into each other, not coffins.

There was no sign of treasure and I soon wished I hadn't come. It was a grim, lonely place. The church clock boomed one o'clock and the ground shook, and here I was, on my own in the vault.

As the sound of the clock died away, I heard another sound. It was faint at first but there was no mistaking it. Men were coming along the passage. I guessed they were smugglers, coming to get the barrels. Even if I wasn't in danger from Blackbeard, the smugglers would surely kill me.

The voices came closer and I was shaking so much I could hardly move. Then I saw a great wooden coffin on a shelf high off the ground. There was a narrow space between it and the wall. So I clambered on to the shelf and squeezed in between the wall and the coffin.

A glow of torches, flickering and red, appeared down the passage. I began to make out the voices. They were talking about Maskew.

'His judgement day'll come,' said a voice I knew, 'and I'll be the judge.'

It was Elzevir Block of the *Why Not?* inn! And Master Ratsey was there with him.

I kept as still as I could and listened. That's all I could do. Then someone else spoke my name and I shivered in my hiding place on the stone shelf.

'I've seen that boy Trenchard hanging round the churchyard. I don't trust him.'

'No need to be afraid of John,' said Ratsey.

'But what if he's spying for Maskew?' said the third voice. 'I say we should get rid of him.'

'He's a good, brave lad,' said Elzevir. 'I wish he were my son.'

It made me proud to hear him say that, but still I dared not move. I stayed there for what seemed like hours until the meeting broke up. Then the torchlight died away and I was left alone.

I waited a moment longer and then began to climb down from the stone shelf. I was stiff from hiding for so long and I lost my balance. I put out my hand to save myself, and the rotten shell

26

of the coffin broke. I looked and saw something like a wisp of seaweed. No, it wasn't seaweed. It was black and wiry… It was a man's beard!

All that time I'd been hiding next to Blackbeard himself!

In a few moments, my terror died down a little and I began to think this was good luck, not bad. I'd found Blackbeard's coffin. Perhaps that would help me find his treasure. I held my breath and gritted my teeth.

I forced myself to look again and saw…a chain and…yes, a locket.

My heart jumped. Surely I'd found the diamond itself. I held the locket to the candle flame and managed to open it. There was nothing inside. Just a piece of folded paper. My spirits fell again. Paper and writing and no treasure.

Perhaps there's some kind of clue on the paper, I thought. I unfolded it and read what was on it.

'The days of our age are threescore years and ten…'

They were verses from the Bible. There was no clue here. Verses wouldn't lead me to the diamond. Blackbeard probably kept them for good luck, to keep evil away.

My disappointment was sharp, but I kept the locket anyway. I gave up all hope of treasure and turned my mind to getting back home before my aunt woke up. I made my way to the end of the passage and there I saw something that filled me with fear. I forgot about hope, I forgot about my disappointment. All I felt now was terror.

The smugglers had put a heavy slab of stone against the entrance and piled earth on top. There was no way out. I was buried alive.

CHAPTER 4

Homeless

I couldn't move the slab, however much I tried. It was solid stone, too large and too heavy. I dug at the earth round the edge, scrabbling with my fingers until they bled, but it was no use. All I managed to do was knock my candle over and lose the light.

Hours went by in darkness. Morning must have come and then gone again. It was too dark to know. I'm sure at least one full day went by. Sometimes I shouted as loud as I could, but there was no one to hear me.

I began to grow weaker and weaker, with hunger and fear and hopelessness. My head started to spin. Everything went blank and I fell to the ground in a heap.

When I next opened my eyes I didn't know where I was. I expected to find dirt and darkness again but I looked round and saw a clean, white room with sunlight at the window. And I was in a bed with clean sheets. I heard a deep voice nearby.

'Here, lad. Drink this.'

I turned my head to see Elzevir Block standing by the bed.

'It's all right,' he said. 'There's no one here to hurt you.'

He told me how I was rescued. Parson Glennie first missed me and went to ask my aunt where I was. She didn't know and she was furious with me. She said that if anyone found me they needn't bother to bring me back to her.

So people started searching, and in the end it was Ratsey who looked in the churchyard. He took me to the *Why Not?*, and here I was, in David's old room. And now I had no other home to go to. All I had with me was Blackbeard's locket and the folded paper with the verses on it. I was still clutching them when they found me. But where I was to go, and how I was to live, I did not know. I think Elzevir saw from my face what I was thinking.

'This will be your home now,' he said. 'You can stay here, lad.'

So the inn became my home, but not for very long. Soon I would lose that, too.

Elzevir rented the inn, and on a certain day every year he had to renew the lease. On that day, the bailiff* called round and Elzevir paid him twelve pounds. Then the *Why Not?* was his for another year. Everyone in Moonfleet knew that Elzevir's family ran the inn and always had. So no one ever bid against him.

This year, though, was different.

The bailiff turned up, as usual, but just as Elzevir was about to hand him the money, the door swung open. We all looked round and in walked Magistrate Maskew. Elzevir jumped up to face him.

'You're not welcome here,' he said.

'I know that, but you can't stop me, Block. I want to take over the inn.'

I could see how much this shocked Elzevir.

'You can't do that,' he said.

'I can and I will. I have every right to make my bid.'

The bailiff told Maskew the inn was Elzevir's home. Did he really mean to take away a man's home? Maskew gave a sour smile. Of course he did. He was a rich man and determined to hurt Elzevir Block, even if it meant paying for an inn he didn't want.

Elzevir made his bid and Maskew bid a little higher. Elzevir offered more and Maskew raised his bid again. And so it went on. We all knew how it would end. It didn't matter who was right. The rich man would get his way. The poor man would lose his home.

And that's what happened.

'Thank you, bailiff,' Maskew said, when the deal was done. 'Master Block, you have till May Day to get out of here for good.'

Now Elzevir had lost the inn, and I had lost my home, we decided to leave Moonfleet altogether. I went to see Grace Maskew, to say goodbye. I was sad to think I might not see her again. Her father was out of the house – I made sure of that.

While I was there I showed her the locket I'd found in Blackbeard's coffin.

'I think it's a clue to where his treasure is hidden,' I said. 'You see the words on this paper? They might be some kind of code.'

Grace did not care about Blackbeard's diamond. In fact, it seemed to make her sad. She asked me not to think about it at all.

'It was got in an evil way and it will bring you no good, John,' she said.

I said I'd always be thinking about her. But I didn't promise to forget the treasure.

Before we said goodbye, I told Grace that when I was out at sea, I used to look up at the Manor House on the hill.

'Sometimes I'd see a candle burning in your room,' I said. 'It was always a comfort to see it.'

'Then I shall keep a candle burning there,' she said with a smile. 'It'll be a light to guide boats at sea.'

After that, she always kept a candle burning at her window. And, in years to come, I was grateful for that light.

A few days before we planned to leave Moonfleet, Elzevir took me aside for a word in secret.

'We have work to do,' he said quietly. 'There are more barrels to be landed.'*

'Now?'

'Tomorrow night. There's a boat coming – the *Bonaventure* – and she'll wait by a little beach along the coast. We'll land the barrels there.'

'And bring them to the place under the church?'

'No. It's not safe there now. Maskew is getting suspicious. I know a cave where we can store them.'

We were alone at the inn at the time, but we spoke in whispers because it was such dangerous talk. It made me nervous, and once I thought I heard a sound at the door. I went outside to look, but the street was empty.

'I thought I heard someone,' I said.

Elzevir laughed. 'The cold has chilled your heart and made you timid,' he said. 'Now get to bed. You won't get much sleep tomorrow night.'

The next night we walked fifteen miles along the coast to meet the others. Our meeting place was called Hoar Head. It was really a steep cliff, a great wall of chalk hanging over the sea. From the top we could just see the *Bonaventure* at anchor in the bay.

'How will we get the barrels up the cliff?' I asked.

'There's a ledge part way down. It's called the under-cliff. It leads down to the beach.'

I followed Elzevir down a track and on to the under-cliff. Ratsey and the others were already there. They had ponies with them, ready for work.

'After tonight, John and I must leave Moonfleet,' Elzevir told the others.

'Ay,' said Ratsey, 'and I shall be right sorry to see you go.'

Just then, there was a low whistle in the distance. Elzevir held up a hand. 'That's the signal,' he said. 'No more talk. We have work to do.'

By the time we got down to the beach a rowing boat from the *Bonaventure* was gliding in to land. We all set about landing the barrels. It was hard work and it must've been three o'clock in the morning before it was done. The *Bonaventure* set sail and slipped silently out to sea again.

We were walking, single file, up to the under-cliff when I caught sight of a movement in the brambles.

'Elzevir! There! Look.'

The others had seen it too, and they were already running towards it. It was a man – a man who'd been watching us – and he was now fleeing for his life. I caught a glimpse of a frightened face looking over his shoulder as he ran. It was Maskew.

'No!' he cried. 'No, for mercy's sake!'

But the men caught him easily and dragged him back. Much as I hated the sight of that face, I had a horrible fear of what would happen next. They threw him to the ground and his pistol fell beside him. Elzevir stepped forward and picked it up.

'Tie him up,' he said. 'Then you can leave him to me.'

They tied Maskew's hands tight behind his back and set him against a block of weatherworn stone. Then they set off along the path, ponies and men, and the three of us were left alone.

'Remember,' said Elzevir, with his face close to Maskew's, 'how you turned me out of my home? Remember how my son was brought back to me dead?'

Maskew begged for his life. He said Elzevir could have his home back. He offered money – a thousand, ten thousand pounds – but Elzevir wasn't listening. He picked up the pistol. The wretch cowered in fear and I thought of Grace, his daughter.

'Please, Elzevir,' I cried and grabbed his arm. 'Let him go!'

'Keep out of this, John!'

Elzevir was a powerful man and he easily shook me off, but as we struggled the pistol went off, firing harmlessly into the air.

Just then, a faint voice came down to us from the top of the cliff. 'Down there, look. On the under-cliff. Three of them.'

I saw the shape of a soldier's hat against the morning sky. Then another. They were peering over the cliff top at us.

'Soldiers!' said Elzevir. 'Quick, run for the cliff!'

Suddenly Maskew yelled out at them. 'Shoot, in the Devil's name! Before he kills me!'

A shot rang out, followed by others. I heard the bullets thud into the turf.

41

We ran and I heard a wild scream behind us. When I looked round, Maskew was slumped over and lying still.

'They've killed him!' I cried.

'Leave him, John. Get close in to the cliff or they'll kill you!'

The next moment, I was on my knees and there was a scorching pain in my left leg. One of the bullets had hit me.

Elzevir picked me up like a child and carried me to the cliff wall.

We were safe, but only for the moment. We could hear the soldiers making their way down the path towards us.

'Can you stand?' Elzevir asked.

'No. My leg hurts too much.'

Above us the soldiers were coming closer.

'They'll be on us soon,' said Elzevir.

'And find us with a discharged pistol and a dead man at our feet. We'll hang,' I cried.

'There is a way to escape, John. It's a sheep track leading up the cliff. It's called the Zigzag. But it's narrow and dangerous, and you're wounded…'

'Let's try it,' I cut in. 'Better to risk falling than to hang at Dorchester Jail.'

Elzevir lifted me on his shoulders and carried me to the Zigzag track. We slunk along, close to the cliff side. It was narrow, sometimes too narrow for Elzevir to hold me. I had to crawl on hands and knees, and trail my injured leg. Then he lifted me on his back again and we struggled a

little further. The effort was terrible.

'Elzevir,' I begged, 'I can't go on! Just leave me. They might have mercy on me.'

'They will not! Keep going. Press close to the cliff, boy, and don't look down.'

The ledge was hardly more than a foot wide. The slightest slip would dash me to the rocks below. My head started to spin. Again we heard the soldiers shout. This time they were below us.

'Look, it's Maskew!'

They were already on the under-cliff and they'd found Maskew's body. They might see us at any moment. So I forgot my fear of falling and dragged myself forward again on hands and knees.

'Brave lad!' said Elzevir.

He glanced back. The soldiers were searching for us, but they hadn't noticed the Zigzag. They raced down the path to the beach. Elzevir laughed when he saw this.

'Now we shall do it, John. We shall do it.'

Five minutes later we stepped on to the cliff top. Below us the sea was a pure blue, with a track of sun across it, all spangled and gleaming.

CHAPTER 5

A puzzle solved

My leg was badly hurt. It would take weeks
to mend. Elzevir took me to a hiding place he
knew in an old marble quarry – Jacob's Pit.
There were shafts cut deep into the rock and in
one of these we made our new home.

It was a gloomy place, though, and water
dripped from the roof. There was a local story
that demons lurked down there.

'Oh yes,' said Elzevir, 'and the worst of them
is the Mandrive. He sneaks up at night and
kills you.' But he was smiling. It was his joke.
I remembered how he'd told me the story of
Blackbeard's ghost in Moonfleet churchyard.

'You must rest now, John. Get some sleep.'

I was worn out with pain so I did sleep. I slept a good long time.

Elzevir made a mash of grass and sorrel* to put on my bad leg and slowly it began to mend. By the time May came, I was able to move again. He then said we should sail on the *Bonaventure*, and start a new life somewhere else.

One evening he went off to make arrangements. He told me to keep my eyes open while he was away.

'If a friend comes,' he said, 'he'll whistle and say the password – *prosper the Bonaventure.*'

Night came on and soon I was lying in perfect darkness. I began to think about the Mandrive, the creature that was supposed to lurk in the tunnels and kill people. To take my mind off it, I lit a candle, took out Blackbeard's locket and looked again at the words on the folded paper.

Suddenly I heard a scratching noise and my candle blew out.

'Who is it?' I asked softly.

There was no answer and I reached for the pistol Elzevir had left me.

'Who goes there? Answer or I fire!'

Then a voice came out of the darkness.

'Prosper the Bonaventure.'

It was Ratsey!

'You hothead,' he said, scrambling over the rocks. 'Would you shoot your best friend?'

He helped me light a fire and then he gave me the news. 'There's a price on your head,[*] John. Twenty pounds, and fifty for Elzevir. You can't stay here much longer. Someone will give you away.'

'We're leaving soon, Ratsey. Elzevir has gone to make the arrangements.'

The fire flickered and he caught sight of the paper in my hand.

'What's this?'

'Verses from the Bible. I was reading them to keep up my courage.'

He took the paper and looked at the words. 'These won't ward off evil spirits,' he said.

'Why not?'

'This wouldn't keep a flea from a black cat.' Ratsey pointed to the numbers of the verses. 'Look,' he went on. 'It says here this is verse twenty-one. Well, that's wrong. It's the tenth verse. They've got all the numbers wrong.'

When Ratsey had gone, I looked at the paper again. It was just as he'd said. The numbers against the verses were wrong. But why? Was there a hidden message?

Then an idea came to me. There were five numbers. Perhaps they were a clue. Perhaps they were there to guide you to particular words. So the number twenty-one meant choose the twenty-first word.

I tried it. I read the paper over and picked out all the words shown by the numbers. This is what it gave me: 'Fourscore* – feet – deep – well – north.'

This, surely, was a clue to Blackbeard's treasure! But what did it *mean?* Was the diamond hidden in a well? If so, where? I'd solved the puzzle but I still didn't know the hiding place.

Elzevir returned and I showed him what I'd worked out. 'Fourscore – feet – deep – well – north.'

It was something to do with a well. All we had to do now was find the right one.

But Elzevir shook his head. 'There's no well that deep round here,' he said.

'There must be. This is where Blackbeard ended his days…'

'True,' said Elzevir, 'but it's not where he got the diamond, is it?'

I thought back to the story of Blackbeard and his royal prisoner in a castle somewhere. King Charles gave him the diamond then.

'It was a castle,' I said, 'but I can't remember where.'

'It was Carisbrooke Castle,' said Elzevir excitedly. 'I've been there many times. It's on the Isle of Wight.'

'And does it have a well?'

'It does, John. Fifty fathoms* or more into the chalk below.'

'So the diamond must be there!'

'If it is,' said Elzevir, 'we shall find it. The *Bonaventure* sails in a fortnight. It can put us down on the Isle of Wight. Then we shall see, lad, then we shall see.'

CHAPTER 6

Deep in the castle

Two weeks later we put to sea. I stood at the rail of the *Bonaventure* and watched Moonfleet disappear behind us. I saw the Manor House on the hill and remembered Grace's promise to keep a candle burning at her window. But with Maskew dead, and a price on my head, I couldn't come back. And that meant I'd never see Grace or her candle again.

We put in at Cowes, on the Isle of Wight, and walked to Newport. We still had to take care we were not discovered, and Elzevir led us to an inn he knew.

'This is the *Bugle*,' he said. 'We'll find friends here.'

He called for the landlord and a man came towards us, wiping his hands on a cloth.

'We're looking for beds and some food,' said Elzevir.

'We're full,' answered the man, turning away. 'Try the *Wheatsheaf*.'

'I can see things *prosper*,' Elzevir added quickly.

The man hesitated. 'What did you say?' he said.

'Prosper.'

'Prosper...what?'

'Prosper the Bonaventure.'

At that the landlord laughed out loud. He'd known Elzevir before, but wasn't sure until he heard the password.

'You're welcome here,' he said. 'Most welcome.'

Elzevir left me at the inn and went for a walk up to the castle.

I was sitting in the little garden at the back of the *Bugle* when he returned. He saw that I was alone so he drew up a chair.

'It won't be easy, John,' he said in a quiet, serious voice. 'The castle is now a prison and it's heavily guarded.'

'What about the well-house?'

'That's guarded too. And the well's so deep they have to use a donkey on a tread wheel to lift the buckets up. The only way we can do this is to get the help of the gaoler. I don't like the look of him, but...well, I had to tell him about the treasure.'

I was surprised he'd told our secret to a stranger.

'I didn't say where it was or how to get it,' Elzevir added quickly. 'But he'll let us in to search for it if we split the treasure three ways.'

A whole third of the value of the diamond! It was a lot to give up, but we had little choice. Elzevir told me the plan. We'd dress as workmen and be at the castle gates at six o'clock next morning. We'd say we were there to plaster up a weak part of the well. The gaoler would let us in, and we'd be there – at the very place where Blackbeard hid his treasure. Simple – as long as nothing went wrong.

We went to the castle next morning and waited
while the gaoler unlocked the iron gates. He was
a rough looking man with shifty eyes. Keeping
his face turned always away from us, he led us
to a square building with a high roof. This was
the well house.

Inside was the well, with a stone wall around it, and a huge wooden wheel nearby. A donkey stood patiently in the wheel. When he walked forward, the wheel turned and a large bucket could be lowered into the well. There was a foot brake to make the wheel slow down or stop.

The gaoler locked the door behind us.

'Why do that?' I asked

'We don't want anyone coming in, do we lad?'

He was right, but I didn't like the idea of being locked in with him.

Elzevir checked Blackbeard's message again: 'Fourscore – feet – deep – well – north.'

'Fourscore' meant the treasure should be eighty feet down the well. Elzevir tied a knot in a rope at the eighty feet mark. Then he got ready to climb into the bucket. I stopped him.

'I'll do it,' I said. 'I'm lighter than you.'

'That doesn't matter, John.'

'Yes, it does,' I said, darting a look at the gaoler. 'I'll go down the well and you stay here to help this gentleman.'

Then Elzevir understood that I didn't trust the gaoler and he agreed. But I could see the gaoler didn't like this arrangement. He told me that going down the well was dangerous. To prove his point he picked up a stone and dropped it into the well. It was a full five seconds before a booming splash echoed back to us. I would be hanging over a long, dark space. But I tried not to think about it and climbed into the bucket.

'Now,' said the gaoler, and he made a clicking noise at the donkey. 'Walk on!'

The donkey set off and the bucket began to sink slowly down the well. The air was damp and chilly, and soon it was as black as night apart from my candle. I looked up and saw the well mouth above me, white and round like a moon.

Then the bucket swung and the rope strained. It had reached eighty feet. I looked at every brick in the wall next to me. But there was nothing.

'It could be the floor,' the gaoler said, far above me. 'It's higher today than it was a hundred years ago.'

'Hold on, John,' called Elzevir. 'We'll lower you down a little.'

The donkey walked, the wheel turned, the bucket swung lower. Suddenly I caught sight of something – a mark scratched on one of the bricks. It was the letter 'Y'! The mark of the Mohunes. Blackbeard's mark!

I took my hammer and chipped away. Soon I was able to slide the brick out and reach behind it. My fingers touched a little bag, parched and dry. I emptied it into my hand and there was a diamond as big as a walnut and flashing with light.

Then, just for a second, I seemed to hear Grace's words in my ear. *It will bring you no good, John.* But I shook my head and shouted up to Elzevir. 'I've found it! Pull me up!'

I went up a lot faster than I'd gone down, but just before I got to the top, the gaoler put the brake on and I was left there, swinging in the bucket.

'Where is it, then?' he said.

'Let the boy up,' Elzevir said. 'It's his treasure.'

'It's not! Listen, I'll give you half shares. Forget the boy.'

'No,' said Elzevir fiercely. 'He'll have his share, or I'll know the reason why.'

The gaoler made a grab at Elzevir and caught his collar. 'I know your name! It's Block, and there's money on your head.* Give me the jewel or I'll hand you over, friend.'

Elzevir broke free. Then I lost sight of both men as they struggled together. Scared that

the gaoler would send the bucket down the well again, I pulled myself up by the rope and climbed out.

The gaoler was struggling with Elzevir close to the wall of the well.

'I'll have you, and your treasure!' he yelled, lunging at Elzevir.

Elzevir blocked his charge and the gaoler staggered backwards.

'Look out!' I cried.

For a moment he stood there waving his arms to keep his balance, then he fell. Elzevir leaped forward and grabbed his belt. He did his best to hold him but the belt began slipping through his fingers.

The man fell and his scream echoed down the well. There was a distant crack and a rumble and wash of water. Then silence.

Elzevir was stunned. 'I had him by the belt, John,' he said. 'I could've saved him.'

'No, Elzevir. No one could. Let's fling the jewel down after him. It brings bad luck.'

'No, give it to me. This man has lost his life for it. Come on. We must get out of here.'

So now there were two deaths and we would be blamed for both of them. We were running away from the Isle of Wight, just as we'd run from Moonfleet. The landlord of the *Bugle* told us there was a Dutch ship ready to sail for Holland. Elzevir said that would be a good place to go because Holland was famous for its diamond markets. We'd be able to sell Blackbeard's treasure.

So we set sail for Holland.

During the voyage, I turned the diamond over and over in my hands. I was glad now that we hadn't thrown it down the well. The way it flashed out bright colours enchanted me. I thought it would make us rich, but Elzevir said he didn't care for riches. The diamond brought bad luck, he said, and he was sick of it.

CHAPTER 7

Stolen!

In Holland, we found a man who traded in diamonds. His name was Aldobrand. A little dried-up man, he was, with yellow skin and deep wrinkles. We told him about our diamond and he led us to a room at the back of his house.

'I hope you don't waste my time,' he said. 'I do not buy rubbish.'

'No, sir. This is a true diamond,' Elzevir told him.

'Then let me see it.'

I tipped the diamond on to Aldobrand's table. For some moments he peered at it closely through an eyeglass.

'What's your name, boy?' he said, at last.

'John Trenchard, sir. From Moonfleet in Dorset.'

He took up a pen and scratched down my name on paper.

Elzevir darted me a look. 'Why do you need to write his name, sir?'

Aldobrand took no notice and went on asking questions. 'And how did you come by this stone, John Trenchard?'

'No,' said Elzevir. 'We're not here to answer questions. We got this diamond fairly.'

'Ah, but this isn't a diamond,' said Aldobrand.
'This is only glass.'

'What?'

'Paste, we call it.'

'You mean it's a fake?' I asked.

'A fake. Worth ten silver crowns, but no more.'

At that Elzevir snatched up the diamond and
said we hadn't come to beg for silver crowns. He
wanted no more to do with it, he said. And he
flung it through the window into the garden.

'No!' shrieked Aldobrand, jumping to his feet.

Elzevir was marching quickly out of the
house. I hurried out after him. He was so angry I
had to run to catch him up.

'Ten crowns!' he said. 'For a man's life!'

'No, Elzevir. Stop!' I took his elbow and made him stop. 'Listen,' I said. 'It is a real diamond. Aldobrand is lying.'

'What? How?'

'He wanted to cheat us and get it for next to nothing. That's why he said it was worthless. But I saw where it fell. Among the flowers. We'll go back and get it.'

Elzevir didn't want to go back. He said we were well rid of it. I told him to think of all the things we could do for the poor people of Moonfleet.

'Please,' I said. 'Let's just go back.'

Later that night we went back to Aldobrand's house. We climbed the wall and dropped quietly into the garden. It was late but Aldobrand was still up. There was a lamp at his window. Elzevir kept watch, while I searched the flowerbeds. I knew exactly where to look. It was close to a red flower…

Yes, there was the flower. I searched the ground all around it. Nothing. No sign of anything…except a very clear footprint in the soil.

'It's gone, Elzevir,' I whispered. 'Aldobrand got here before us!'

'Then let that be the end of it, John! Let's just go…'

'But he's stolen it!' I cried. 'I won't leave until I've seen what he's up to.'

I scrambled up towards the room with the light in it. I meant to climb up to the window and see what Aldobrand was doing.

It wasn't easy, but I was determined. The room had wooden shutters and they were closed, but I managed to find an opening and peer in.

I saw Aldobrand sitting there with my stone – the queen of all diamonds in the world.

Elzevir had climbed up behind me, and now I heard his voice.

'Come away,' he whispered. 'Forget the diamond.'

I took no notice.

Then Aldobrand left the room and I saw my chance. I was trying to undo the wooden shutters when I lost my balance and fell. I crashed into the room, sprawling on the floor. My head was ringing with the sound of bells. It was Aldobrand's alarm system. He'd set up wires to trigger bells all over the house.

In seconds he came charging back into the room, shouting, 'Thieves! Thieves!'

'I'm no thief!' I cried. 'I've only come for what is mine!'

Running into the room behind him came five or six servants with sticks and clubs. Elzevir leaped to my side, and the servants attacked us both. I felt a crack on the side of my head and I fell to the floor.

They threw us into a stone cell. Our ankles were chained and there was only stinking straw to lie on. All this was my fault! I cursed myself for being so foolish but Elzevir never said a word against me.

We were taken to court and Aldobrand swore that we attacked him and stole the diamond. No one listened to our story and we were sentenced to the galleys* for life.

As we were taken away, I shouted, 'Good day, Sir Aldobrand, liar and thief. May the diamond you took from us bring you all the bad luck you deserve!'

And that was the end of our freedom. We were chained together with other prisoners in groups of six, our wrists fixed to a long bar. Elzevir went with one group and I went with another. I saw him led away and then I saw him no more.

CHAPTER 8

Paying the price

I was marched to a place called Ymeguen and
set to work building a fortress. It was hard work
in terrible conditions. They branded us with a
hot iron to show we were prisoners. We were
marked with the letter of the place where we
worked – a 'Y' for Ymeguen.

It reminded me of the 'Y' in the coat of
arms of the Mohunes, back in Moonfleet – an
unlucky letter from the start.

So years passed, of endless work and bad
food, and I grew from boy to man. Then one
day, my work was changed.

I was handed over to a party of soldiers, to be put on a ship for Java in the East Indies.* In Java they had sugar farms and they were sending out hundreds of prisoners to work like slaves. A hot, distant country where I would die.

We were trudging along in a line, heading for the ship. Ahead of me was a prisoner with a shock of white hair and bowed shoulders. I couldn't see his face but I began to think I knew him from somewhere.

'Elzevir?' I said quietly, and the prisoner turned round. '

'John.'

He had changed a great deal – he looked much older and he was much more worn – but it was certainly my old friend.

My heart lifted to know we were together again. I tried to ask how he was but the guards wouldn't let us talk.

'Silence, there!' they shouted. 'March! We board ship tonight!'

We were forced into the hold of a ship and the hatches were shut on us. We could see nothing but we sensed the ship had left harbour for the open sea. It began to rock and creak with

the blow of a storm. In the hold, it was wet and dark, no better than a pigsty, but at least we were able to talk.

'Is this what it has come to, Elzevir?' I said. 'To live and die a slave? Can you ever forgive me?'

'No point blaming yourself, John,' he answered. 'At least we are together again.'

We had been brought up near the sea. We were used to its harsh ways. Some of our fellow prisoners weren't. As the ship tossed in the storm, they groaned and called out for help.

'It's getting lively out there,' I said.

'If it goes on like this,' said Elzevir, 'we won't ever reach Java.'

He was right. For about a week we sailed into the storm. Then the gale became worse. We could hear the wind screaming through the rigging. We could feel the ship plunge wildly.

Suddenly, the hatch opened, letting in a splash of salt water. Our guard's face peered in. He flung a key down to us and disappeared. He was giving us a chance to save our lives.

We undid our chains and struggled on to the deck. It was thick night and the sea was raging all around us. There was no sign of the crew.

'They've taken the boats!' shouted Elzevir. 'They've left us!'

A wave crashed down on us and white water foamed across the deck. Through the darkness I could make out a line of land. We were close to some shore and the storm was forcing us inland.

'Can you see?' I cried. 'Is it cliff or sand?'

'Cliff, look! High above!'

I looked hard through the driving rain and

saw the shape of the cliff. And I knew it. I knew that stretch of coast! I knew its every line from the days of my boyhood.

'Elzevir! Look! We're in Moonfleet Bay!'

And so we were. There was only a mile between us and home. But it was a mile of death. The sea battered the land, and I could see no way through. I felt Elzevir grab my arm.

'Johnnie, I'd rather drown on Moonfleet beach than live in some prison. Let's make a fight for life!'

'How?'

'Steer the ship straight for the beach!'

'But we can't see, Elzevir! We can't even see the beach!'

We had to see what we were doing – otherwise we would be wrecked for certain. Just then we caught sight of a tiny light blinking through the rain.

'Look!' said Elzevir. 'A light! It's the Manor House. That's Maskew's old place!'

Then I knew what it was – the candle burning at Grace's window. All those years had passed and still she kept it lit.

'Steer for the light!' Elzevir cried as we struggled to keep the ship heading for the beach. 'When the next big wave takes us close, we jump. Goodbye, John, and God save us both!'

The next wave came down like a fist. The air was full of the roaring of the sea and the smashing of timber.

◆◆◆

Silence.

I didn't know how much time had passed. I didn't know where I was. I opened my eyes and saw I was in a room with a fire burning gently in a grate. Then I heard a voice in the room.

'There, friend, there. Don't move.'

A dark figure was leaning over me.

'These walls,' I said. 'I know where I am. I'm in the *Why Not?*'

'Yes,' said the figure, with some surprise. 'So you are. You know the name?'

'I do,' I said, and struggled to sit up. 'Elzevir…where is Elzevir?'

'What?'

'Please, tell me where he is!'

The figure looked at me, frowning, as if he knew me but couldn't believe it. I could see his face clearly now.

'Don't you know me, Master Ratsey?' I said.

'John?' he said softly. 'John Trenchard?'

'Yes, Ratsey, it's me. Where's Elzevir?'

'Elzevir Block hasn't been seen here since…'

'But we were together. He landed with me.'

'That was Elzevir who dragged you out of the sea?' Ratsey said, amazed. 'I saw him catch the rope we threw but I couldn't see his face.'

Then I began to remember…

The surge of the sea. Elzevir reaching out his hand. Our fingers touching.

'You were swept down the beach again,' said Ratsey, 'and…oh, brave heart, he was, such a brave heart.'

Then Ratsey told me how Elzevir went back into the sea to save me. He was clear of danger but he went back for my sake. He walked back into the very jaws of death, Ratsey said, to rescue me. Then the sea got hold of him and dragged him off his feet again.

'We didn't see him after that.'

'No!' I cried. 'I must find him, Ratsey!'

Weak as I was, I got to my feet and went down to the beach to look for my friend.

The beach was covered in wreckage from the ship. The sea was littered with splintered wood. There was no sign of Elzevir. I sat down at the top of the beach, with my head between my hands, and stared out to sea.

Ratsey came looking for me.

'He will come in, Ratsey,' I said quietly. 'Everything comes back to the beach in the end.'

It was midday, under a thin and watery sun, when the first body was washed ashore. Three others followed soon afterwards. Then I saw one roll over in the surf and knew at once that it was Elzevir.

Ratsey helped me pull him out of the running foam. I wrung the water from his hair and wiped his face and, kneeling, held him in my arms.

We carried him up to the inn and laid him down on the table. It was the same table where his son David had been laid out. His face was hardly marked and he had a look of great peace about him. We covered him with a sail, and Ratsey left us alone for a while.

I was now a free man again but what use was freedom to me? My friend had gone.

When it was dark, Ratsey came back to the inn and brought someone with him. It was the parson, my old schoolteacher, Mr Glennie.

'They told me of your sorrow, John,' he said, and then sat beside me while the fire burned and the light dimmed.

After a while, Mr Glennie said there was something he had to tell me. 'I had a letter, John, about eight years ago.'

'A letter? What is it?'

'It was from a lawyer in Holland. He had a message to give me from a Mr Aldobrand.'

'Him,' I said bitterly.

'Aldobrand made a will. He said he once took a diamond without paying the proper price for it. He said he wanted to ask John Trenchard of Moonfleet to forgive him. He wanted to pay him back.'

'He wanted to pay me?'

'Yes. You are to be rich. But I hope you'll use your fortune well, John.'

'Don't worry, Mr Glennie,' I said. 'I've learned a bitter lesson over this. A bitter lesson.'

It was midnight when Mr Glennie left me. Then I heard someone else step into the room. I didn't turn until I felt a light touch on my shoulder.

'John,' said a voice, 'have you forgotten me?'
It was Grace Maskew.

'Did you see the light, John? Did you know
I was waiting for you in Moonfleet? Have you
forgotten?'

So I became a rich man. But I never touched a
penny piece of this wealth. I spent it all on new
homes for the poor folk of Moonfleet.

Elzevir has a grave on the sunny side of the
church, and Grace and I now live in this our
happy Moonfleet. We love to walk along the
cliffs and see the sea spread out below us, always
the same and always changing.

But I love the sea best when it's lashed to madness during a storm. I hear the roar of the waves and the churn of pebbles on Moonfleet beach. And then I remember my dear friend Elzevir and the night he gave his life to save me.

J Meade Falkner

(born 1858, died 1932)

John Meade Falkner was born in Manningford Bruce, Wiltshire. His father was the village curate (assistant to the vicar). When he turned five, his mother started giving him lessons in Latin, and from his sixth birthday, his father taught him Greek. He went to school in Dorchester and the headmaster at the time was Ratsey Maskew – names Falkner would later use for two characters in *Moonfleet*. He later moved with his family to Weymouth, Dorset.

Falkner studied at Oxford, then became a private tutor to the Armstrong family, who ran one of the largest weapons manufacturing companies in the world. Falkner became a successful businessman and the chairman of this company during World War I.

Falkner married when he was 40, but had no children. He spoke several modern languages, as well as Latin and Greek.

Falkner wrote only three novels, including *Moonfleet*. His other two works of fiction were *The Lost Stradivarius* and *The Nebuly Coat*. He also published several volumes of poetry and guides to Oxfordshire, Bath and Berkshire.

Nick Warburton

Nick taught in primary schools for ten years before becoming a full time writer. Among his children's novels are *The Thirteenth Owl*, *Normal Nesbitt*, *Lost in Africa* and *You've Been Noodled*. His stage plays are *Touch Wood* and an adaptation of *Farmer Giles of Ham*.

Nick has also written and adapted plays for radio, including the *Peter Pan* sequel, *Peter Pan in Scarlet* by Geraldine McCaughrean. His television work includes scripts for *Doctors*, *EastEnders*, *Born and Bred* and *Holby City*.

Nick has also run courses on creative writing, and has chaired the judging panel for the Writer's Guild of Great Britain's children's book award.

About *Moonfleet* he says, 'It's a fast-paced story and as exciting as *Treasure Island* (considered to be one of the greatest adventure yarns of all time). *Moonfleet* isn't all fights and chases, though. There's a mystery with a secret code, underground dens and danger at sea. (I love sea stories.) I also find that I care about the characters and the pain and loss they suffer. I first heard the story on the radio, when I was a teacher marking books in the staff room. Years later I turned the story into a radio play (which you might still find on a BBC cassette somewhere) and now I'm very pleased to have the chance to write this version.'

Notes about this book

The fictional village of Moonfleet was set in Dorset, where Falkner spent much of his childhood. Some of the places described in the story are based on real locations. Moonfleet itself is a village called Fleet near Chesil Beach – the longest pebble beach in Europe, stretching for 18 miles west of Weymouth. Hoar Head, where John is shot in the leg by a soldier, is believed to be the high cliff called White Nothe to the east of Weymouth.

The smuggling which lies at the heart of the story was still a recent memory in Falkner's time and, indeed, may have been continuing when he wrote the story. At the time of the story, in the latter half of the 18th century, it would have been a way for fishermen to make some extra money, although a risky one, as the penalties were harsh if they were caught.

Page 5
*aground When a ship is driven by wind or currents on to the beach or rocks.

Page 6
* smugglers People who try to bring goods like alcohol or tobacco into the country from overseas without paying tax to the government on the smuggled goods.

Page 7
*magistrate A member of the legal profession who acts as a judge in local courts. Magistrates have the power to pass sentence on people found guilty of breaking the law.

men from the Revenue Goverment officials from the Customs department, part of whose job it is to try to catch smugglers.

Page 9
parson The priest at the local church.
coat of arms The symbols of an individual or a family (usually rich) that were displayed on decorative shields.

Page 12
backgammon A board game for two people involving moving pieces at a throw of the dice.

Page 17
unearthly Something which cannot be explained by everyday experience.

Page 23
tinderbox An old device used before the invention of matches to start fires and light pipes.

Page 33
bailiff A person who has legal power to perform certain actions, such as collecting rent and debts.

Page 36
'...to be landed' To be brought from a ship on to land.

Page 47
sorrel A herb with healing qualities.

Page 48
'a price on your head' If you are wanted by the authorities and they offer a reward for your capture, then you have 'a price on your head'.

Page 50
****fourscore** A score is another way of saying 20, so fourscore is 80 (4 times 20).

Page 51
****fathoms** Old unit of measurement for the depth of the sea. A fathom is six feet, or about two metres.

Page 59
****'money on your head'** Means the same as 'a price on your head'. (See note for page 48 above.)

Page 69
****galleys** Large single-decked wooden ships, powered by sails and a large number of oarsmen who were often prisoners, doing it against their will.

Page 71
****East Indies** A term used to describe India, Indonesia and islands in South East Asia. In the 1600s to mid 1800s, the English and the Dutch set up companies to trade their manufactured goods, such as cotton, for local produce and goods, like spices.